SPLISH SPLASH!

by Ethel and Leonard Kessler

Parents' Magazine Press
New York

*

Library of Congress Cataloging in Publication Data
Kessler, Ethel.
  Splish splash!
  SUMMARY: Describes the progressive signs of spring
from the melting of winter's ice to the appearance of
the ice cream man.
  [1. Spring—Poetry] I. Kessler, Leonard P., 1920-
joint author. II. Title.
PZ8.3.K44Sp   811'.5'4   72-8137
ISBN 0-8193-0654-1   ISBN 0-8193-0655-X (lib. ed.)

For Adrianne, Christopher, Connie,
Deborah, Derrick, Diane, Glennise,
James, Janine, Jarrod, Jennifer,
John, Karen, Kristin, Laura, Marlo,
Matthew, Melissa, Michael, Patrick,
Richard, Rita, Selma, and Louis

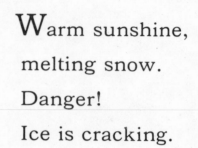

Warm sunshine,
melting snow.
Danger!
Ice is cracking.

Ice is melting
on a winter pond.
Where is winter?
Winter's gone!

No more
ear muffs,
big boots,
furry hats,
snow suits,
heavy scarves,
warm mittens,
no more snow!
Splish — splash!
Where did it go?

Down below

into the ground

it goes

to wake sleeping seeds

that climb and grow.

Splish — splash.

It's spring!

Turtle sleeping
in the soft wet mud,
wake up!
It will soon be time
to lay your eggs.
Wake up,
it's spring!

Hey in there,
brown bear,
wake up!
Can't you tell,
can't you smell
it's spring!

Hey, sleepy head,
get out of bed.
Wake up,
it's spring!

Still in bed,
sleepy head?
Feel the warm breeze.
Sleeping buds open
on thin, bare trees.
Wake up,
it's spring!

O-ka-lee! O-la-lee!

The redwings sing

a song of early spring.

Walk in the low
wet woods
where the first
skunk cabbages grow.

Touch the soft and furry
catkins of the
gray pussy willows.

Snow white crocus
peek at me.
White blossoms hang
on shadbush trees.

The cold ponds
and quiet woods
are quiet no more.
Newborn bugs
buzz and hum
in the early spring.
Buzz-buzz-buzzzzzzzz.
Tiny peepers
loudly whistle
Peep. Peep. Peep.
Catch a bug.
Eat a bug.
Peep. Peep. Peep.

Honk. Honk.
Quack. Quack.
The ducks and geese
are flying back,
quietly gliding
into the pond.
Splish—splash!

Robins are looking
for little twigs,
straw, mud,
bits of string,
to build their nests
in the early spring.

Spring is yellow,
spring is green,
and every color
in between.
The tiny tips
of young green grass
push through
the soggy ground.

There are yellow
golden daffodils,
buttercups on windy hills,
the smell of lilacs fills
the air.
The smell of spring
is everywhere.
I can smell the spring.

I can hear
the sounds of spring...
a scolding squirrel,
the robin's cheerful,
bubbling song,
a frog croaking,
rain dripping.
SPLISH! SPLASH!

April showers
wash my face.
I step over a puddle.
I jump
into the middle
of a great big puddle.

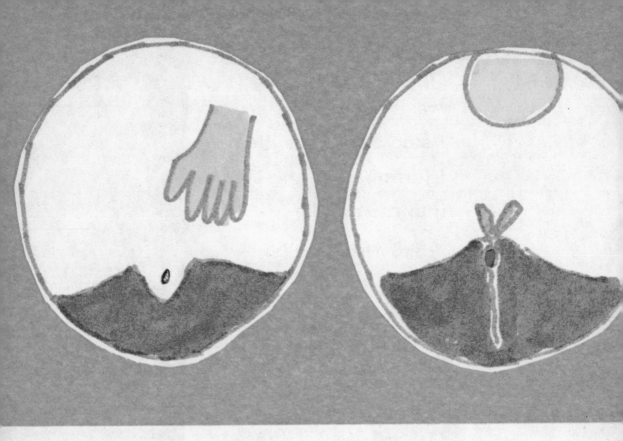

In the spring

I plant

a tiny seed in the ground.

I pile a little soil

around the seed.

Pat. Pat.

Just like that.

The sun and rain

and water

will make it grow.

What will it be?

Do you know?

Not a carrot,

not a weed.

I just planted a...

radish seed.

I can sing a song of spring...
"A tadpole is a polliwog.
A polliwog becomes a frog."

I can sing
a silly song
of spring…
"Fiddle dee dee.
Fiddle dee dee."

…the fly has married the bumble bee ….

Ring-a-ling,
ring-a-ling.
I know that sound
that comes in the spring.
It's the ice cream man,
and what does he bring?

I scream.

You scream.

We all scream

for

ICE CREAM.

I run through
the fresh cut grass
without my shoes.
It tickles my toes.

Dandelion seeds

that blow in the breeze

tickle my nose

and make me

sneeze.

AAChoo!

AAChoo!

Bye and bye,

summer sky.

Splish — splash!

Spring is gone.

Splish — splash!

Keep cool.

Splish—splash!

jump in the pool.

SPLISH

SPLASH!